Going on a Plane

by Alison Sage

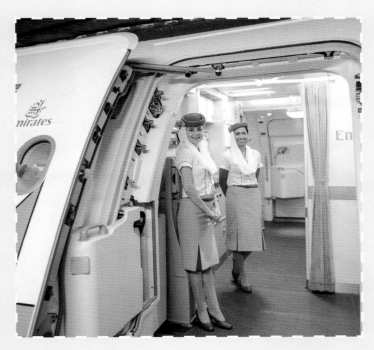

Contents

CAMBRIDGE
UNIVERSITY PRESS

UCL
Institute of Education

At the airport

Going by plane is an amazing way to travel.
Every day, 9 million people fly around the world.

Big airports can look like a city. They are very busy places.

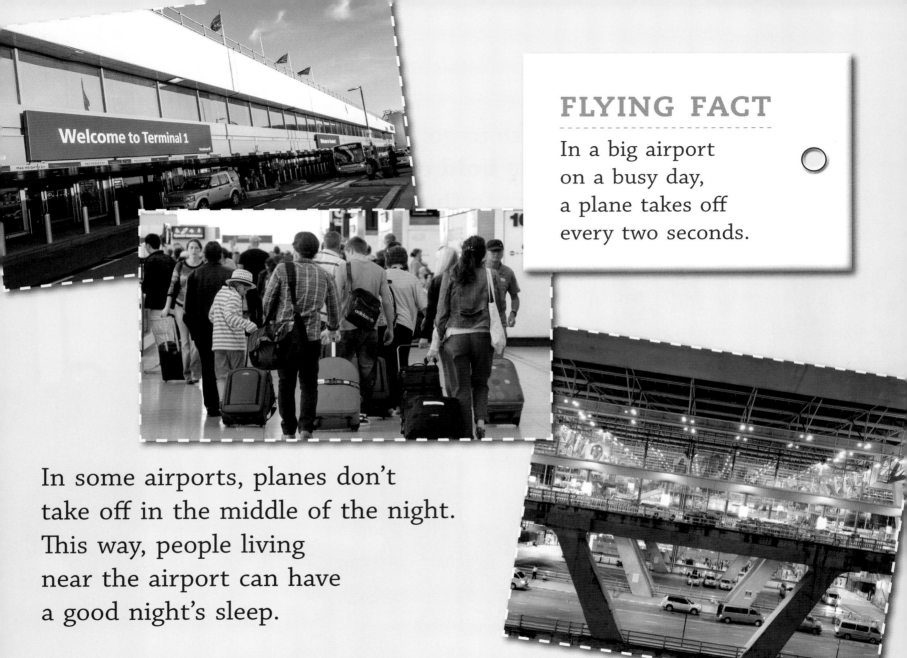

In a big airport
on a busy day,
a plane takes off
every two seconds.

Welcome to Terminal 1

In some airports, planes don't
take off in the middle of the night.
This way, people living
near the airport can have
a good night's sleep.

3

Checking in

The **check-in** is the first place to go. **Passengers** hand in their heavy bags. These go into the **hold** of the plane. Passengers can take a small bag with them onto the plane.

small bag

big bag

name and address

This label shows where the bag is going.

Big bags go onto a **conveyor belt**.
Then they are put in a truck, ready
to be taken to the plane.

*In Heathrow airport,
London, there are 20 miles
of conveyor belts.*

Airlines use computers to track
bags anywhere in the world.

Departures

All the small bags must now go through a **scanner**.

The person in charge of the scanner can see what is inside each bag.

When all their small bags have been checked, passengers can go into the **departure lounge**. This is where everyone is waiting for their **flight**.

There are lots of cafes and shops.

Some shops are open all night.

Sometimes you can see planes taking off and landing.

This Airbus 380 can carry over 500 passengers.

This moving walkway makes walking easy. But look out when it stops!

Everyone seems to be in a hurry in an airport.

There is also a long way to walk.

Getting on the plane

Passengers are boarding their plane. The **flight attendant** is there to welcome everyone.

This flight is showing on the information board.

An **airbridge** is fixed to the plane while the passengers get on.

There are rows and rows of seats. The flight attendant tells the passengers where to sit.

Some people like to look out of the window as the plane takes off.

overhead lockers for bags

window

seat belt

Flight attendants make sure everything in the cabin is ready for take-off. They also are there to help if a passenger is ill.

This is the air crew.

The pilot is called the captain and he is in charge of the plane. There is also a **co-pilot**.

These are flight attendants. They look after the passengers.

The **cockpit** is where the pilots sit.

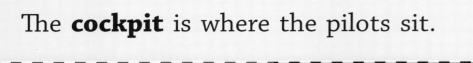

computer screens

joystick

throttle

Before a plane takes off, it needs fuel. This fuel tanker is on its way to **refuel** a plane.

The fuel tanks are underneath the plane.

FLYING FACT

○ A Boeing 747 uses 1 gallon of fuel every second.

The truck is carrying the passengers' bags to be loaded onto the plane.

This crane lifts the containers into the cabin.

A truck carries all the food and drinks for the flight in boxes called containers.

in-flight meals

15

Take-off!

The flight attendant shows the passengers how to fasten their seatbelts.

She gives out sweets to suck. This is to stop the passengers' ears feeling funny when the plane goes up in the air.

It's time for take-off!

The engines roar and the plane begins to race down the **runway**.

In the air

When the plane is in the air, passengers can play a game or watch a film.

Later, the flight attendant brings everyone a meal.

The flight attendant gives out puzzles and games to children.

Some people want to walk about. They go to the toilet if they want to.

19

Landing

The pilot begins speaking: 'We will be landing in fifteen minutes,' he says.

The plane is going down. There are houses, roads and a city below.

They look bigger, and bigger, and bigger.

Soon, the plane lands on the runway.

The flight attendant says goodbye to the passengers as they leave the plane.

Glossary

check-in: place in the airport where passengers give their bags and get their boarding passes

cockpit: place in plane where the pilot and co-pilot sit

conveyor belt: moving transporter

co-pilot: person who helps fly a plane

crane: machine that lifts heavy things.

flight: air trip

flight attendant: person who looks after passengers on a plane

hold: place for big bags on plane

passengers: people who are travelling in a vehicle

refuel: fill with fuel again

runway: long area where planes land and take off from

scanner: machine for seeing what is inside bags

Index

Going on a Plane Alison Sage

Teaching notes written by Sue Bodman and Glen Franklin

Using this book

Developing reading comprehension

Plane travel may well be something with which the children are familiar. This book offers the opportunity to revisit some of the things they will have experienced, or to introduce plane travel to children who have yet to do so. Written predominantly as a report, the text offers some chronology in the sequencing of events, more in keeping with explanatory texts. Non-fiction text features such as captions, labels and facts boxes support comprehension.

Grammar and sentence structure

- Language structures and verb tenses are in keeping with the genre, for example: generic features of report-writing: *'passengers', 'some airports'*; chronology of explanation *'When the plane is in the air ...', 'soon the plane lands ...'*.

- Longer, more complex sentences, including the use of connectives to join clauses: *'The flight attendant says goodbye to the passengers as they leave the plane.'* on page 21.

Word meaning and spelling

- Reading of novel or unfamiliar multi-syllabic words (*'conveyor', 'departure'*) using the context and glossary to ensure the meaning is understood.

- Spelling of present tense verb endings (*'says', 'tells', 'brings'*) and the use of auxiliary verbs (*'everyone is waiting', 'passengers are boarding', 'we will be landing'*), noting the spelling of the /ing/ inflection on the main verb.

Curriculum links

Geography – Use a map to chart where in the world the children have travelled.

Science – Children could experiment with different designs of paper planes. What is the best paper to use? What helps the planes to fly further or to stay in the air longest?

Learning Outcomes

Children can:

- use non-fiction features to support understanding of the text

- adapt to the language of non-fiction texts, using the language structures and grammatical conventions of the genre

- attempt unfamiliar words, using known syllable chunks, monitoring that their meaning is understood.

A guided reading lesson

Book introduction

Begin with a discussion about plane travel – which children have been on a plane? Ask them to share their experiences and be prepared to discuss your own.

Orientation

Give each child a copy of the book. Ask them to read the title and the blurb. Ask them to tell you whether it is a fiction or a non-fiction text, taking you to sections in the book to demonstrate reasons for their answers.

Say: *In this book, we can read all about going on a plane. I wonder if some of the things we discussed will be in here.* Look quickly down the contents page and link to the prior discussion.

Preparation

Ask the children to read pages 2 and 3 quietly to themselves and discuss some of the facts described, such as that 9 million people fly every day and that a plane takes off every two minutes (in the Flying Facts box on page 3).

Pages 4 and 5: These pages offer a good opportunity to explore a range of non-fiction features: labels captions, facts boxes and glossary words. Spend time exploring the use of these with the children. Look at the word *'conveyor'* on page 3. Practise breaking this into syllables, using decoding skills, and then check the meaning of *'conveyor belt'* in the glossary.